WHEN ADULTS ALIGN

By

Ethan L. Ketterer

WHEN ADULTS ALIGN

Printed in USA

First Edition

ISBN: 978-8 -9999942-1-9

For professional development, speaking engagements, or inquiries, contact:
admin1@mykturn.com

DEDICATION

Dedicated to the educators, paraprofessionals, teaching assistants, and leaders who understand that student success begins with adult alignment.

To those who are willing to reflect honestly, adjust intentionally, and commit to working together even when it is difficult.

Your professionalism, consistency, and shared responsibility shape classrooms and schools where students experience clarity, stability,

and the opportunity to succeed.

AUTHOR'S NOTE

Over time, it became clear that many of the challenges facing students are not rooted in curriculum, resources, or intent but in adult misalignment. In schools where adults work hard yet operate without shared expectations, consistent language, or unified direction, students experience confusion long before they experience content.

I have worked in educational spaces where adult alignment was strong and I have worked in spaces where it was not. In each setting, the difference was visible in student behavior, classroom climate, and overall school culture. What students experienced daily was not just instruction, but the quality of adult collaboration surrounding them.

This book is not written from theory alone. It is grounded in lived classroom experience across roles that are often separated by title but united by responsibility. It reflects conversations that are frequently avoided, dynamics that are rarely named, and behaviors that quietly shape outcomes.

When Adults Align is not about perfection. It is about clarity.

It is about recognizing that students respond first to adult behavior long before they respond to lessons, systems, or interventions. When adults are aligned in expectations, professionalism, and purpose, students benefit from consistency, stability, and trust.

This book does not seek to assign blame or elevate one role above another. Instead, it invites reflection, shared ownership, and intentional alignment across classrooms and schools. The goal is not uniformity, but unity grounded in respect, accountability, and commitment to student success.

If this book challenges you, that is intentional. Growth often begins with discomfort. If it affirms what you already practice, let it strengthen your resolve. And if it offers language for what you have felt but struggled to name, use it to start conversations that move your school forward.

Alignment is not accidental.
It is chosen daily.

My hope is that this book serves as both a mirror and a guide, encouraging adults to align their actions, expectations, and purpose in ways that create stronger environments for students to learn and thrive.

TABLE OF CONTENT

INTRODUCTION

Why Adult Alignment Can No Longer Be Optional

Before students encounter instruction, they encounter adults.

They encounter adult tone, adult expectations, adult consistency, and adult behavior. Long before a lesson is taught or an intervention is implemented, students are reading the environment around them watching how adults interact, respond, support, and align.

And they respond accordingly.

In schools where adults are aligned, students experience clarity. Expectations are predictable. Boundaries are consistent. Support feels coordinated. In schools where adults are misaligned, students experience confusion often before they experience content. Mixed messages replace clarity. Inconsistency replaces structure. And learning competes with uncertainty.

This book begins with a simple but often overlooked truth:

Students respond first to adult alignment or the lack of it.

Good Intentions Are Not Enough

Most educators care deeply about students. They work hard, show up consistently, and do their best under demanding conditions. Yet despite good intentions, many schools struggle with fractured culture, inconsistent expectations, and uneven student outcomes.

The issue is rarely effort.
It is alignment.

When adults operate with different expectations, language, and responses—often unintentionally students are left to navigate the gaps. Behavior escalates. Trust weakens. Climate suffers. And the focus shifts from learning to management.

Good intentions alone cannot overcome misalignment.

What Students Experience When Adults Are Not Aligned

Students do not need to understand school structure to feel its effects.

They notice:

- When expectations change from room to room
- When rules are enforced inconsistently
- When adult responses contradict one another
- When tension exists between staff

These experiences shape how students engage, behave, and trust the environment. Misalignment teaches students that expectations are negotiable and authority is divided whether or not that is the message adults intend to send.

Alignment is not about control.
It is about clarity.

Alignment Is a School wide Responsibility

Adult alignment is often treated as an individual classroom issue rather than a collective responsibility. Yet alignment cannot be sustained in isolation.

A single aligned classroom inside a misaligned system will always struggle. Students move between rooms, adults, and expectations. What they experience across the school matters just as much as what happens inside one space.

This book shifts the focus from individual effort to collective responsibility because alignment must exist **across adults**, not just within them.

This Is Not a Book about Compliance

When Adults Align is not about micromanagement, rigid uniformity, or stripping educators of autonomy. Alignment does not require sameness. It requires shared direction.

Alignment means:

- Shared expectations
- Consistent professional behavior
- Clear communication
- Mutual accountability

It allows individuality within a framework that students can trust.

Why This Conversation Is Often Avoided

Adult alignment is uncomfortable to discuss.

It requires:

- Honest reflection
- Willingness to examine behavior
- Courage to name inconsistencies

For this reason, alignment issues are often reframed as student problems, curriculum gaps, or policy failures. While those factors matter, they cannot compensate for adult misalignment.

Avoiding this conversation does not protect schools—it weakens them.

What This Book Offers

This book provides a clear, practical framework for understanding how adult alignment shapes student experience and school culture.

You will explore:

- How adult behavior sets the tone for learning
- Where and why alignment breaks down
- The hidden cost of inconsistency
- How power dynamics affect unity
- What alignment looks like in daily practice
- How leaders protect and sustain alignment
- How alignment can be repaired when it fractures

This is not a quick fix. It is a realistic guide grounded in real school dynamics.

Who This Book Is For

This book is written for:

- Classroom teachers
- Paraprofessionals and teaching assistants
- Instructional teams
- School leaders and administrators

It is for those willing to reflect honestly and commit to improvement—not perfection.

The Choice Ahead

Alignment does not happen by accident.

It is built through shared language, consistent behavior, and collective accountability. It is sustained through intention, reflection, and willingness to adjust.

The question is not whether adult alignment matters.

The question is whether schools are willing to treat it as essential.

Moving Forward

The chapters that follow challenge long-held assumptions and invite a shift in perspective—from individual classrooms to collective culture.

Because when adults align, students benefit.

And when students benefit, everything else becomes possible.

CHAPTER 1

Why Adult Alignment Matters More Than We Admit

E very school has expectations.
Every classroom has rules.
Every educator has intentions.

Yet student experience is shaped less by what is written and more by what is lived.

Adult alignment is the invisible force that determines whether expectations feel clear or confusing, whether boundaries feel stable or negotiable, and whether students experience school as predictable or fragmented. While alignment is often discussed in passing, its impact on students is far greater than many schools are willing to acknowledge.

This chapter begins with a necessary truth:

Adult alignment is not a supporting factor in student success it is a determining one.

What Students Experience Before Instruction

Before students engage with curriculum, they engage with consistency or the lack of it.

They observe:

- How adults speak to one another
- How rules are enforced
- How tone shifts across spaces
- How quickly expectations change

These observations shape student behavior long before instruction begins. When adults are aligned, students experience clarity. When adults are misaligned, students experience uncertainty.

Uncertainty does not create learning-ready environments. Clarity does.

Alignment Is Felt, Not Announced

Schools often communicate expectations clearly—to adults.

But students experience alignment through action, not intention.

Alignment is felt when:

- Expectations are reinforced consistently
- Adults support one another publicly
- Responses are predictable across situations
- Boundaries remain steady

When alignment is missing, students receive mixed messages. Mixed messages invite testing. Testing invites escalation. Escalation pulls attention away from learning.

This pattern is not accidental. It is predictable.

Why Misalignment Is So Common

Misalignment rarely comes from neglect. It comes from complexity.

Schools are busy, demanding environments where:

- Adults work under pressure
- Roles vary widely
- Communication is often rushed

- Time for alignment is limited

In these conditions, adults may default to individual judgment rather than shared direction. Over time, this creates variation in expectations, tone, and response.

The result is not intentional harm it is unintended inconsistency.

The Hidden Cost of "That's Just Their Style"

One of the most common phrases used to excuse misalignment is:

"That's just their style."

While individual style matters, it cannot override student need for consistency.

When "style" determines expectations:

- Students must constantly adjust behavior
- Boundaries feel negotiable
- Authority feels divided

Alignment does not erase individuality but it does require shared foundations. Students should not have to relearn expectations every time they encounter a new adult.

Misalignment Creates Extra Work for Everyone

When adults are misaligned, workload increases.

Teachers spend more time managing behavior.
Support staff spend more time clarifying expectations.
Administrators spend more time addressing preventable issues.

Misalignment creates inefficiency. Alignment creates flow.

Aligned adults spend less time reacting and more time teaching.

Why Alignment Is Often Underestimated

Adult alignment is often underestimated because its absence is normalized.

Schools adjust to misalignment by:

- Increasing interventions
- Adding systems
- Creating new policies

Yet these solutions rarely address the root issue. Without adult alignment, even the best systems struggle to function.

Alignment is foundational—not optional.

What Alignment Actually Means

Alignment does not mean sameness.

It means:

- Shared expectations
- Consistent language
- Unified responses
- Professional consistency

Adults can differ in personality, teaching style, and approach while still aligning on what matters most for students.

Alignment provides the structure within which individuality can thrive.

Alignment Is a Collective Responsibility

Alignment cannot rest on individual classrooms alone.

Students experience schools as systems. What happens across hallways, transitions, and interactions matters as much as what happens within a single room?

When alignment is treated as optional or isolated, inconsistency spreads. When alignment is treated as collective responsibility, culture strengthens.

The Impact on Students

When adults align, students experience:

- Predictability
- Safety
- Clear boundaries
- Fairness

These conditions support learning, trust, and engagement.

Alignment does not guarantee success but its absence guarantees struggle.

A Shift in Perspective

This chapter asks for a shift in how schools think about alignment.

Not as:

- A preference
- A leadership style
- A compliance issue

But as:

- A student experience issue
- A cultural responsibility
- A daily practice

When adults align, students benefit in ways that are both immediate and long-lasting.

Moving Forward

The chapters that follow will explore:

- Where alignment breaks down
- Why good intentions are not enough
- How alignment can be built and sustained
- The role each adult plays

Because alignment is not accidental.

It is chosen—daily.

Reflection & Application

- Where does alignment feel strong in your school?
- Where does inconsistency show up most often?
- What expectations do students experience differently depending on the adult present?

Honest reflection is the first step toward alignment.

CHAPTER 2

Students Respond to Adult Behavior First

B efore students respond to expectations, they respond to people.

They respond to tone before rules. They respond to consistency before consequences.

They respond to how adults behave long before they respond to what adults say.

In schools focused on curriculum, pacing guides, and outcomes, this reality is easy to overlook. Yet student behavior, engagement, and trust are shaped first by adult conduct—not instructional intent.

This chapter centers on a foundational truth:

Students mirror adult behavior before they internalize adult expectations.

Behavior Is a Response to Environment

Student behavior does not exist in a vacuum.

It is shaped moment by moment by:

- How adults speak to students
- How adults speak to one another
- How calmly or reactively adults respond to challenges
- How predictable adult behavior feels across settings

Students are constantly scanning their environment for cues. Those cues come primarily from adult actions, not adult explanations.

When adult behavior is steady, students regulate more easily.
When adult behavior is unpredictable, students compensate—often through testing, withdrawal, or resistance.

Uncertainty invites behavior.
Clarity reduces it.

Tone Teaches Faster Than Words

Tone is instructional.

Students learn quickly from:

- The emotional energy adults bring into interactions
- Whether correction feels calm or confrontational
- Whether expectations are delivered with respect or frustration

A calm tone communicates safety.
A reactive tone communicates instability.

Even when the words are appropriate, tone determines how students receive the message. Students may not remember exactly what was said, but they remember how it felt.

Tone teaches students what to expect next.

Consistency Is the Foundation of Trust

Students do not require perfection from adults—but they do require consistency.

Consistency tells students:

- Expectations are real
- Boundaries are predictable
- Adults can be trusted

Inconsistent adult behavior communicates uncertainty. When expectations change depending on who is present, students are forced to adjust constantly. This adjustment often shows up as testing limits, negotiating rules, or disengaging altogether.

Consistency is not rigidity.
It is reliability.

Students Track Inconsistency Instantly

Adults may view inconsistency as minor. Students do not.

They notice:

- When one adult enforces a rule and another overlooks it
- When consequences vary widely for the same behavior
- When tone shifts dramatically across spaces

This does not make students manipulative it makes them adaptive.

Students adapt to inconsistency by experimenting. They test where boundaries hold and where they do not. What appears as defiance is often a response to unclear adult alignment.

Adult Reactions Shape Student Regulation

Students frequently borrow regulation from adults.

When adults:

- Pause before responding
- Maintain composure under pressure
- Address issues calmly and consistently

Students learn how to regulate their own emotions.

When adults:

- React emotionally
- Escalate quickly
- Contradict one another publicly

Students mirror that instability.

Adult regulation teaches student regulation—whether intentionally or not.

Why Students Behave Differently for Different Adults

It is common to hear statements such as:

- "They never act like this for me."
- "They know better."
- "They behave when they want to."

In reality, students are responding to different adult cues.

Different adults may communicate:

- Different tolerance levels
- Different emotional energy
- Different follow-through

Students adjust behavior accordingly. This is not manipulation—it is pattern recognition.

When adult behavior is aligned, students no longer need to adjust.

The Emotional Climate Is Always Teaching

Students do not separate academics from emotion.

They experience classrooms as emotional environments shaped by adult behavior. When adults are tense, rushed, or disconnected, students feel it. When adults are calm, respectful, and aligned, students feel that too.

Emotional climate influences:

- Willingness to engage
- Risk-taking in learning
- Behavior regulation
- Trust in adults

Adult behavior sets that climate daily—often before instruction begins.

Alignment Strengthens Adult Authority

There is a misconception that alignment weakens individual authority. In practice, the opposite is true.

When adults respond consistently:

- Expectations feel fair
- Boundaries feel solid
- Correction feels purposeful rather than personal

When adults contradict one another:

- Authority feels negotiable
- Boundaries feel optional
- Correction feels arbitrary

Aligned authority is stronger, not weaker.

Modeling Is Constant even in Small Moments

Students are always learning even when adults are unaware they are teaching.

They learn:

- How frustration is handled
- How conflict is addressed
- How mistakes are responded to
- How respect is demonstrated

These lessons are absorbed quickly and remembered long after specific content is forgotten.

Adult behavior is curriculum.

Why Alignment Begins With Adult Self-Awareness

Alignment does not begin with policies.
It begins with awareness.

Adults must reflect on:

- Tone during stress
- Consistency of responses
- Emotional reactions
- Follow-through

Self-awareness is not self-criticism. It is responsibility.

Students cannot be expected to regulate behavior in environments where adult behavior is unpredictable.

What Aligned Adult Behavior Looks Like in Practice

Aligned adult behavior includes:

- Predictable responses across adults
- Calm, respectful correction
- Shared language around expectations
- Professional consistency

This does not mean perfection. It means intentionality.

Aligned behavior creates clarity—even during correction.

A Necessary Shift in Perspective

This chapter invites a shift from asking:

"Why are students behaving this way?"

To asking:

"What are students responding to?"

That shift reframes behavior from a problem to be managed into information to be understood.

Understanding opens the door to alignment.

Moving Forward

The next chapter explores what happens when adult intentions are good—but messages are mixed.

Because adult behavior may be unintentional, but its impact is never neutral.

Reflection & Application

- How might students describe adult behavior across your school?
- Where does tone or consistency differ most between adults?
- What behaviors do adults unintentionally model during moments of stress?

WHEN ADULTS ALIGN

Awareness is the first step toward alignment.

CHAPTER 3

When Good Intentions Create Mixed Messages

Most misalignment in schools does not come from neglect or lack of care. It comes from good intentions that are not coordinated.

Educators across roles enter schools wanting the same thing: students who feel supported, respected, and capable of success. Teachers, paraprofessionals, teaching assistants, and leaders often share the same goals yet students still experience inconsistency, confusion, and unpredictability.

This chapter explores a difficult but necessary truth:

Good intentions, when unaligned, can still create mixed messages for students.

Intent does not automatically translate into clarity. Without alignment, even the best intentions can unintentionally undermine the learning environment.

Intent and Impact Are Not the Same

Intent reflects what adults *mean* to communicate.
Impact reflects what students actually *experience*.

When adults are aligned, intent and impact move together.
When adults are misaligned, a gap forms—and students
live in that gap.

An adult may intend to:

- Be supportive
- Show grace
- Reduce conflict
- Build relationships

Yet students may experience:

- Unclear expectations
- Inconsistent boundaries
- Uneven consequences
- Conflicting authority

Impact shapes behavior far more than intent. Students
respond to what feels predictable, not what is meant to be
helpful.

How Mixed Messages Appear in Daily Practice

Mixed messages are rarely dramatic. They appear in everyday moments that feel insignificant to adults but meaningful to students.

They show up when:

- A rule is enforced in one classroom and ignored in another
- A behavior is corrected by one adult and dismissed by another
- Tone varies drastically across spaces
- Expectations are explained differently depending on who is speaking

Individually, these moments may seem minor. Collectively, they shape student understanding of what actually matters.

Students begin to ask—often unconsciously:

- "Which adult means it?"
- "Who will follow through?"
- "Where are the real boundaries?"

Flexibility without Alignment Becomes Confusion

Flexibility is often praised in schools and rightly so. Students benefit from adults who are responsive and thoughtful.

But flexibility without alignment creates confusion.

Flexibility is:

- Intentional
- Communicated
- Coordinated

Inconsistency is:

- Unintentional
- Unspoken
- Fragmented

When one adult adjusts expectations without shared understanding, students are left guessing. What one adult views as compassion, another may experience as undermining expectations.

Without alignment, flexibility loses its supportive purpose.

The Power of Unspoken Assumptions

Many mixed messages originate from assumptions adults do not realize they are making.

Common assumptions include:

- "Everyone knows what we mean by this expectation."
- "We all handle this the same way."
- "If no one said anything, it must be fine."

Assumptions replace clarity with silence. Silence creates space for misinterpretation.

What is unspoken is rarely shared—and what is not shared cannot be aligned.

Conflicting Signals Students Pick Up Immediately

Students are highly perceptive observers of adult dynamics.

They notice:

- When an adult corrects a student and another adult intervenes differently
- When an expectation is reinforced publicly in one moment and contradicted in another
- When adults disagree quietly but behave inconsistently

Even subtle cues tone, body language, timing signal whether adults are aligned.

When adults send conflicting signals, students test which message holds authority.

Why Avoidance Creates More Confusion

Alignment conversations are often avoided to preserve comfort.

Adults may avoid:

- Addressing differences in approach

- Clarifying expectations
- Naming inconsistency

Avoidance may feel easier in the moment, but it transfers the burden to students. Instead of adults resolving differences, students are forced to navigate unclear expectations.

Avoiding alignment does not prevent discomfort.
It simply moves it downstream.

Students Test What Is Unclear

Students do not test boundaries to be defiant.
They test boundaries to find clarity.

When messages are mixed:

- Students experiment with behavior
- They observe which adults follow through
- They adapt responses based on patterns

This behavior is often mislabeled as manipulation. In reality, it is problem-solving in an inconsistent environment.

Students test until expectations become clear.

Unity Does Not Require Agreement on Everything

Alignment does not mean adults must agree on every approach or preference.

It does mean adults agree on:

- Core expectations
- Non-negotiable
- How correction is handled
- How adults support one another publicly

Adults can disagree privately and still present unity publicly. That unity provides students with stability even during correction.

Unity communicates safety.

From Individual Judgment to Shared Direction

When adults rely solely on individual judgment, inconsistency increases.

Shared direction provides:

- Predictability for students
- Reduced behavioral testing
- Clear boundaries across settings

Shared direction does not eliminate professional autonomy. It creates a framework within which autonomy can function effectively.

Students thrive when autonomy exists inside alignment.

Aligning Intentions Requires Intentional Conversation

Alignment does not happen through proximity.
It happens through communication.

Effective alignment requires adults to:

- Name expectations explicitly

- Discuss differences honestly
- Clarify gray areas
- Agree on shared responses

These conversations require professionalism and humility. They are not signs of dysfunction they are signs of commitment.

What Aligned Intentions Look Like in Practice

When adult intentions are aligned, students experience:

- Consistent language
- Predictable responses
- Clear boundaries
- Unified authority

Impact improves when intention is shared, clarified, and coordinated.

A Necessary Shift

This chapter calls for a shift from assuming alignment to actively building it.

Good intentions matter but only when they are aligned.

Without alignment, even the most caring environments become confusing.

Moving Forward

The next chapter examines what happens when mixed messages become systemic and the cost of inconsistency across classrooms.

Because misalignment does not stay contained.
It spreads.

Reflection & Application

- Where students might be receiving mixed messages across your school?

- What assumptions might adults be making without realizing it?
- Which conversations would strengthen alignment if they happened?

Alignment begins when intentions are no longer private but shared.

CHAPTER 4

Inconsistent Expectations across Classrooms

Inconsistency is one of the most powerful and unintended teachers in a school.

When expectations vary from classroom to classroom, students learn quickly. Not necessarily the rules, but how flexible those rules are. They learn where boundaries hold, where they bend, and where they disappear entirely. Over time, inconsistency reshapes student behavior, adult authority, and school culture in ways that are often underestimated.

This chapter addresses a difficult but necessary reality:

Inconsistent expectations across classrooms create confusion for students and additional strain for adults.

What may feel manageable in isolation becomes harmful when experienced across an entire school day.

How Inconsistency Becomes Normalized

In many schools, inconsistency is not intentional it is tolerated.

It often sounds like:

- "Everyone runs their room differently."
- "That's just their teaching style."
- "As long as learning is happening."

While autonomy matters, unexamined variation creates an uneven experience for students. Over time, inconsistency becomes normalized, and its impact goes unchallenged.

What adults accept quietly, students absorb daily.

Students Experience Schools as Systems, Not Silos

Students do not experience schools one classroom at a time.

They experience:

- Transitions
- Hallways

- Multiple adults
- Shifting expectations

A student may follow one set of rules in the morning, a different set by mid-day, and yet another by dismissal. Each adjustment requires cognitive and emotional effort.

Inconsistent expectations increase cognitive load. Increased cognitive load reduces learning capacity.

The Behavioral Cost of Inconsistency

Inconsistent expectations create predictable behavioral responses.

Students may:

- Test limits more frequently
- Argue rules
- Negotiate expectations
- Become disengaged or withdrawn

This behavior is often labeled as defiance. In reality, it is adaptation.

Students adapt to inconsistent environments by searching for clarity. When clarity is missing, behavior fills the gap.

Why "They Know Better" Is Not Enough

Adults often respond to inconsistent behavior by saying:

- "They know better."
- "They're choosing to act this way."

Knowing expectations is not the same as trusting them.

When expectations are enforced unevenly, students learn that rules are conditional. Trust erodes. Compliance becomes situational.

Behavior is shaped less by knowledge and more by predictability.

How Inconsistency Weakens Adult Authority

Authority is strongest when it is collective.

When students see:

- Different rules in different classrooms
- Different consequences for the same behavior
- Adults correcting each other publicly

Authority feels fragmented. Boundaries feel negotiable.

Aligned expectations shift authority from individual enforcement to collective structure. Students respond more consistently when authority feels shared.

The Impact on Collaboration between Adults

Inconsistency affects adults as much as it affects students.

It creates:

- Frustration when expectations are undermined
- Tension between classrooms
- Increased referrals and escalations
- Strained relationships among staff

When expectations are unclear, adults are forced into reactive roles instead of collaborative ones.

Inconsistency quietly erodes trust between adults.

Autonomy vs. Fragmentation

Autonomy allows educators to bring creativity and responsiveness into their classrooms.

Fragmentation occurs when autonomy is disconnected from shared expectations.

Autonomy without alignment leads to:

- Confusion
- Uneven enforcement
- Mixed student experiences

Alignment provides the foundation that allows autonomy to function without fragmentation.

Students thrive when flexibility exists inside consistency.

Why Systems Alone Cannot Fix Inconsistency

When inconsistency becomes visible, schools often respond by adding systems:

- New behavior frameworks
- Additional documentation
- Tiered interventions

While systems matter, they cannot compensate for inconsistent adult behavior.

No system overrides daily inconsistency.

Alignment is the system beneath all systems.

What Consistent Expectations Actually Require

Consistency does not mean identical classrooms or rigid control.

It requires:

- Shared non-negotiable

- Common language around behavior
- Predictable responses to key behaviors
- Collective follow-through

These elements create stability while preserving professional autonomy.

Consistency is collaborative, not controlling.

The Role of Leadership in Expectation Alignment

Inconsistent expectations are rarely resolved without leadership involvement.

Leadership must:

- Name inconsistency clearly
- Facilitate alignment conversations
- Protect shared expectations
- Model consistency

When leadership avoids alignment conversations, inconsistency persists.

Alignment requires protection, not assumption.

Reframing Inconsistency as a Student Experience Issue

This chapter calls for a necessary reframe.

Inconsistent expectations are not:

- Personality differences
- Teaching preferences
- Harmless variation

They are:

- Student experience issues
- Cultural indicators
- Collective responsibilities

When expectations are inconsistent, students pay the price first.

Choosing Consistency without Control

Consistency does not require micromanagement.

It requires:

- Agreement
- Communication
- Ongoing reflection

When adults align expectations intentionally, consistency becomes supportive rather than restrictive.

Moving Forward

The next chapter examines how power, position, and silence quietly protect misalignment—and how those dynamics deepen division across schools.

Because inconsistency is rarely accidental.
It is often sustained by unspoken systems.

Reflection & Application

- Where do expectations differ most across classrooms in your school?
- Which inconsistencies are most visible to students?

- What shared non-negotiable would immediately reduce confusion?

Consistency begins when adults choose alignment over isolation.

CHAPTER 5

Power, Position, and Silent Division

Not all misalignment announces itself.

Some of the most damaging divisions in schools are quiet—rooted in power, position, and what goes unspoken. These divisions rarely appear in meeting agendas or policy documents, yet they shape daily interactions, influence whose voice matters, and determine how consistently expectations are upheld.

This chapter addresses a difficult but necessary truth:

When power dynamics go unexamined, alignment fractures—and silence protects the fracture.

Power Is Present Whether We Name It or Not

Power is not inherently negative. It is a reality of any organization.

In schools, power shows up through:

- Job titles and contracts
- Decision-making authority
- Access to information
- Proximity to leadership
- Longevity and experience

These dynamics influence who feels comfortable speaking, who feels expected to comply, and whose perspective shapes school norms.

Ignoring power does not remove it.
It simply allows it to operate without accountability.

How Power Shapes Alignment—Quietly

Alignment requires shared direction. Power often determines whose direction becomes the default.

When power dynamics are unexamined:

- Expectations may be set without full collaboration
- Feedback may flow in only one direction
- Some adults feel empowered to challenge decisions
- Others feel pressure to remain silent

Over time, alignment becomes uneven. Some adults help shape expectations, while others are expected to enforce expectations they had no role in defining.

Alignment built on imbalance is fragile.

The Silent Division between Roles

In many schools, division forms quietly between roles.

Teachers, paraprofessionals, teaching assistants, and support staff may share the same space but not the same influence. When certain roles are consistently excluded from conversations about expectations, behavior, or systems, alignment becomes partial.

Silence fills the space where dialogue should exist.

That silence often looks like:

- Unasked questions
- Withheld observations
- Quiet compliance
- Private frustration

Silence should never be mistaken for agreement.

Why Silence Feels Safer Than Honesty

Many adults remain silent not because they lack insight, but because speaking feels risky.

Silence may feel safer when:

- Past feedback was dismissed or minimized
- Power feels uneven or unclear
- Professional consequences feel uncertain
- Relationships feel fragile

Silence becomes a protective strategy—but it undermines alignment.

Alignment cannot grow where honesty feels unsafe.

How Students Perceive Power Dynamics

Students are highly perceptive observers of adult behavior.

They notice:

- Who sets expectations
- Whose corrections stand
- Whose authority is reinforced
- Whose decisions are questioned

When power dynamics are inconsistent, students learn quickly which adults "count." This shapes how they respond to redirection, boundaries, and consequences.

Fragmented authority creates fragmented compliance.

Undermining Authority—Often Without Intention

Authority is not always undermined through confrontation.

It is often undermined quietly through:

- Contradicting an adult publicly

- Reversing decisions without discussion
- Ignoring expectations set by others
- Using tone or timing to signal disagreement

Even subtle undermining weakens alignment. Students learn where authority truly lies by watching adult interactions.

Public unity protects authority.
Private disagreement protects professionalism.

The Cost of Avoiding Power Conversations

Power conversations are often avoided to preserve comfort.

Yet avoidance allows:

- Resentment to grow
- Mistrust to deepen
- Misalignment to harden

When power goes unaddressed, it becomes invisible—but still active.

Avoidance does not protect relationships.

It erodes them.

Leadership's Role in Addressing Silent Division

Alignment across power lines does not happen on its own.

Leadership plays a critical role by:

- Inviting voices across roles
- Creating psychologically safe spaces
- Naming power dynamics respectfully
- Protecting honest dialogue

When leadership avoids these responsibilities, silence persists.

Alignment requires intentional inclusion—not assumption.

Shared Authority without Losing Structure

Addressing power dynamics does not mean flattening all structure.

It means:

- Clarifying roles and decision-making boundaries
- Valuing contributions across positions
- Reinforcing collective authority

Shared authority strengthens alignment when it is guided and intentional. Students benefit when adults operate as a unified system rather than a hierarchy of competing voices.

From Silent Compliance to Shared Responsibility

Alignment grows when silence is replaced with conversation.

That requires:

- Trust
- Professional respect
- Willingness to listen
- Commitment to shared outcomes

When adults feel safe to speak, alignment becomes possible.

Shared responsibility replaces quiet resentment.

A Necessary Reframe

This chapter invites a reframe.

Power dynamics are not:

- A personal flaw
- A single-role problem
- An unavoidable reality

They are:

- A cultural condition
- A shared responsibility
- An opportunity for growth

When power is acknowledged and addressed, alignment strengthens rather than fractures.

Moving Forward

The next chapter examines what happens when misalignment and power dynamics turn into open or hidden conflict—and the cost that conflict carries for students.

Because unresolved adult division never stays contained. It shows up where students live and learn.

Reflection & Application

- Where might power dynamics be influencing alignment in your school?
- Whose voices are consistently heard—and whose are quiet?
- What conditions would make honest conversation safer?

Alignment requires courage—not silence.

CHAPTER 6

Adult Conflict and Its Hidden Cost to Students

Adult conflict rarely stays adult.

Whether it is visible or subtle, addressed or avoided, conflict between adults reshapes the emotional climate of a school. Students feel it before it is explained. They respond to it before it is resolved. And they carry its effects into classrooms, hallways, and learning spaces.

This chapter confronts a reality schools often minimize:

When adult conflict goes unresolved, students experience instability even when the conflict is never discussed openly.

Conflict Does Not Need to Be Loud to Be Harmful

When people think of conflict, they often imagine confrontation raised voices, visible arguments, or formal complaints. In schools, conflict is more often quiet.

It shows up as:

- Avoidance instead of conversation
- Shortened or transactional communication
- Passive resistance to shared expectations
- Inconsistent follow-through
- Emotional withdrawal or detachment

These behaviors may feel manageable to adults, but they are not neutral. Quiet conflict changes how adults interact and students notice.

Silence does not mean resolution.
It often means tension without repair.

How Conflict Alters the Learning Environment

Students do not need context or explanation to sense division.

They notice:

- Shifts in tone between adults
- Hesitation or uncertainty during correction
- Adults avoiding one another
- Mixed signals about authority

These cues communicate instability. When students sense adult tension, they become more alert and less regulated. Their focus shifts from learning to monitoring the environment.

Instruction may continue, but safety and predictability are weakened.

The Emotional Weight Students Should Not Carry

Students often absorb emotional weight that does not belong to them.

When adults are in conflict:

- Students may feel pressure to align with certain adults
- Authority feels divided rather than collective
- Boundaries feel unclear
- Trust in the environment weakens

Students may respond by acting out, withdrawing, or attempting to mediate adult dynamics. None of these responses support learning.

Students should never be responsible for managing adult relationships.

Why Conflict Is Often Avoided

Adult conflict is frequently avoided for understandable reasons.

Adults may avoid addressing conflict because:

- Time feels scarce
- Relationships feel fragile
- Power dynamics feel uneven

- Fear of escalation or retaliation exists

Avoidance may feel protective in the moment. Over time, it deepens division and allows resentment to harden.

Unaddressed conflict does not disappear.
It settles into patterns that shape culture.

Conflict and Inconsistency Are Closely Linked

Conflict and inconsistency often reinforce one another.

When adults are in conflict:

- Communication decreases
- Alignment weakens
- Expectations drift

Students experience this drift as unpredictability. The same behavior may receive different responses depending on adult relationships rather than shared standards.

Inconsistency is often the visible symptom of unresolved conflict.

Healthy Disagreement vs. Harmful Conflict

Disagreement is not the problem.

Healthy disagreement:

- Is discussed openly
- Centers on ideas, not individuals
- Leads to clearer understanding
- Strengthens decision-making

Harmful conflict:

- Is avoided or personalized
- Undermines trust
- Weakens alignment
- Impacts student experience

Schools need disagreement to grow. They do not need unresolved conflict to persist.

What Students Learn From Adult Conflict

Students learn constantly from adult behavior especially during tension.

They observe:

- Whether adults address issues directly or avoid them
- Whether disagreement is handled respectfully
- Whether repair follows conflict

These observations become lessons about communication, accountability, and relationships.

Adult conflict is instruction even when unintended.

When Conflict Becomes a Leadership Responsibility

Unresolved conflict rarely resolves without leadership support.

Leadership plays a critical role by:

- Noticing shifts in collaboration

- Creating space for resolution
- Setting expectations for professional conduct
- Protecting respectful dialogue

When leadership avoids conflict, silence becomes normalized and division deepens.

Alignment requires leaders who are willing to enter discomfort for the sake of stability.

Repair Is a Professional Responsibility

Repair does not require agreement on every issue.

It requires:

- Acknowledgment of tension
- Willingness to communicate
- Commitment to shared outcomes
- Respectful re-engagement

Repair restores stability for students even when adults continue to hold different perspectives.

Public repair protects student trust.

What Repair Looks Like in Practice

Repair may involve:

- Clarifying expectations that drifted
- Addressing misunderstandings directly
- Resetting communication norms
- Reaffirming shared commitments

Repair does not erase conflict.

It prevents conflict from defining culture.

The Cost of Ignoring Repair

When repair does not happen:

- Misalignment deepens
- Authority fragments
- Student behavior escalates
- Adult morale declines

Over time, unrepaired conflict becomes embedded in daily practice.

Repair is not optional.

It is foundational.

Reframing Conflict as Opportunity

This chapter invites a necessary reframe.

Conflict is not:

- A failure of professionalism
- A weakness to be hidden
- A distraction from real work

It is:

- A signal that alignment needs attention
- An opportunity to strengthen trust
- A moment to model resolution

Handled well, conflict strengthens culture.
Avoided, it weakens it.

Moving Forward

The next chapter marks a shift from understanding breakdown to building intentionally.

It explores how shared language and direction reduce conflict before it begins.

Because alignment is sustained through structure not hope.

Reflection & Application

- Where unresolved adult conflict might be affecting students in your school?
- How conflict is typically handled or avoided among adults?
- What would repair look like in one strained professional relationship?

Conflict does not define a school.

How adults respond to it does.

CHAPTER 7

Shared Language, Shared Direction

A lignment does not begin with agreement. It begins with language.

Before adults can move together, they must speak with intention. In schools where alignment struggles, the issue is often not effort or care but language that varies just enough to confuse students and fragment direction. Adults may believe they are aligned because goals sound similar, yet students experience inconsistency because the language guiding expectations is different.

This chapter establishes a central truth:

Shared language is the bridge between intention and action. Without it, alignment cannot be sustained.

Language Is the First System Students Encounter

Before students encounter rules, procedures, or consequences, they encounter words.

They hear:

- How adults describe expectations
- How behavior is corrected
- How mistakes are framed
- How accountability is communicated

Language is the first system student's experience and often the most influential. When language varies, systems feel unstable. When language is shared, systems feel coherent.

Culture lives in language long before it lives in handbooks.

Why Similar Words Are Not the Same Language

One of the most common alignment misunderstandings is assuming that similar words mean shared meaning.

For example:

- "Respect"
- "Appropriate behavior"
- "Accountability"
- "Making good choices"

Without shared definitions, these words become placeholders rather than anchors. Each adult fills them with personal meaning, shaped by experience, role, and preference.

Students are left to decode expectations rather than internalize them.

Shared language requires shared meaning not just shared vocabulary.

How Inconsistent Language Trains Students to Negotiate

When language is inconsistent, students quickly learn that expectations are flexible.

They begin to:

- Ask different adults the same question
- Reference what another adult allows
- Challenge correction using comparative language

Statements such as:

- "They don't care in that class."
- "That's not what I was told."
- "You didn't say it like that yesterday."

These responses are not manipulation. They are evidence that students are responding to inconsistency.

Shared language removes the incentive to negotiate.

Shared Language Is a Tool for Equity

Inconsistent language often impacts students unevenly.

When expectations are unclear or inconsistently communicated:

- Some students receive repeated correction
- Others receive leniency

- Bias intentional or not has more room to operate

Shared language reduces subjectivity. It provides students with clear, predictable expectations regardless of who is speaking.

Consistency is not just about order it is about fairness.

What Shared Language Sounds Like Across Roles

Shared language must cross roles, not just classrooms.

A student should hear similar language from:

- Classroom teachers
- Paraprofessionals and teaching assistants
- Hall monitors
- Office staff
- Administrators

When language aligns across adults, students experience continuity. When it does not, students experience fragmentation even if expectations are technically the same.

Alignment must travel with the student.

Direction Turns Language into Action

Language without direction becomes polite noise.

Shared direction answers:

- What do we prioritize when expectations conflict?
- What behaviors require immediate, unified response?
- What flexibility is appropriate and when?

Direction clarifies when adults should act individually and when they must act collectively.

Language names expectations.
Direction enforces them.

From Individual Judgment to Collective Clarity

Without shared language and direction, adults rely on individual judgment.

Individual judgment leads to:

- Inconsistent enforcement
- Increased adult conflict
- Student confusion

Collective clarity does not remove professional discretion it guides it.

Students do not need adults to respond identically.
They need adults to respond predictably.

Why Shared Language Must Be Practiced, Not Posted

Shared language cannot live only in documents.

It must be:

- Practiced aloud
- Reinforced consistently
- Modeled publicly
- Corrected when it drifts

Posting expectations without practicing language creates performativity alignment rather than lived alignment.

Students learn from what adults say repeatedly not what is written once.

Leadership's Role in Sustaining Language and Direction

Shared language requires protection.

Leadership must:

- Model aligned language consistently
- Reinforce language during moments of stress
- Address drift respectfully and promptly
- Ensure all roles are included

When leadership language drifts, alignment erodes quickly.

Consistency from leadership stabilizes language across the building.

Language during Stress Reveals Alignment

Alignment is most visible during moments of stress.

During conflict, crisis, or disruption:

- Does language remain consistent?
- Do adults revert to personal phrasing?
- Are expectations reinforced or softened unpredictably?

Stress reveals whether language is internalized or merely agreed upon.

Shared language that holds under pressure builds trust.

Why Shared Language Reduces Adult Conflict

Many adult conflicts are not disagreements about values— but about interpretation.

Shared language:

- Reduces misunderstanding
- Clarifies intent
- Prevents public contradiction

When adults speak the same language, conflict decreases because expectations are no longer personal they are collective.

Alignment protects relationships.

Alignment Is Maintained Through Repetition

Shared language is not achieved it is maintained.

Maintenance requires:

- Repetition
- Reflection
- Reinforcement

Drift is natural. Re-alignment is intentional.

Schools that revisit language regularly sustain alignment longer than those that assume it will hold on its own.

A Cultural Shift, Not a Script

This chapter does not call for robotic speech.

It calls for cultural clarity.

Shared language creates:

- Stability for students
- Confidence for adults
- Consistency across spaces

When adults speak with shared purpose, students move with greater trust.

Moving Forward

The next chapter builds on this foundation by examining **professionalism as the stabilizing force** that protects alignment especially when stress, emotion, or disagreement threatens to pull adults apart.

Because language sets direction.
But professionalism keeps it intact.

Reflection & Application

- What words are used most often to correct behavior in your school?

- Where does language vary the most across adults?
- Which shared phrases would immediately reduce confusion for students?

Alignment grows when language is intentional and direction is shared.

CHAPTER 8

Professionalism as a School wide Standard

Alignment does not survive on agreement alone. It survives on professionalism.

Shared language and direction create clarity but professionalism protects that clarity when stress, emotion, disagreement, and pressure enter the building. Without a shared understanding of professionalism, alignment weakens precisely when it is needed most.

This chapter establishes a critical truth:

Professionalism is not an individual preference it is a collective standard that safeguards alignment and protects student experience.

Why Professionalism Cannot Be Left to Interpretation

Professionalism is often treated as subjective something each adult defines based on personality, experience, or role. In schools, this approach creates inconsistency.

When professionalism is individually defined:

- Tone varies widely
- Boundaries shift unpredictably
- Responses escalate unnecessarily
- Alignment erodes under stress

Students experience professionalism not as intention, but as behavior. What adults' model publicly becomes the standard students trust or question?

Professionalism must be shared to be effective.

Professionalism Is Most Visible Under Pressure

Anyone can appear professional when conditions are calm.

Professionalism is revealed when:

- A student challenges authority
- Behavior escalates unexpectedly
- Adults disagree
- Time is limited
- Emotions are heightened

These moments expose whether professionalism is internalized or per formative. Students watch closely during stress. They learn whether adults can remain consistent when it matters most.

Professionalism under pressure creates stability.

Tone Is a Professional Tool

Tone is one of the most powerful indicators of professionalism.

A calm, measured tone communicates:

- Control
- Respect
- Predictability

A reactive tone communicates:

- Instability
- Personalization
- Loss of alignment

Even when expectations are correct, tone determines whether students experience correction as fair or emotional.

Professional tone supports authority without escalation.

Timing and Presence Matter

Professionalism is not only what adults say it is when and how they say it.

Professional presence includes:

- Addressing issues promptly, not publicly
- Choosing moments that preserve dignity
- Remaining emotionally regulated

Poor timing undermines even the best intentions. Students read presence as much as language.

Professionalism protects dignity for everyone involved.

Professionalism Preserves Collective Authority

Authority weakens when professionalism slips.

Public disagreement, sarcasm, dismissive responses, or visible frustration fracture adult unity. Students interpret these cues quickly and adjust behavior accordingly.

Professionalism:

- Protects adult unity
- Reinforces collective authority
- Prevents students from navigating divided systems

Aligned authority is strongest when professionalism is consistent.

Public Unity and Private Resolution

One of the clearest markers of professionalism is how adults handle disagreement.

Professional schools:

- Address differences privately
- Present unity publicly
- Protect student confidence

This does not require agreement on every issue. It requires commitment to resolution without disruption.

Students should never be placed in the middle of adult disagreement.

Professionalism Must Extend Across Roles

Professionalism is not role-specific.

Students interact with:

- Teachers
- Paraprofessionals
- Teaching assistants
- Administrators
- Support staff

When professionalism varies by role, alignment fractures. Students benefit when professionalism looks and sounds consistent regardless of title.

Alignment requires shared standards across positions.

Boundaries Are a Professional Responsibility

Professionalism includes maintaining appropriate emotional and relational boundaries.

This means:

- Avoiding venting in front of students
- Keeping adult conflict out of student spaces
- Managing frustration privately

Boundaries protect students from adult stress they are not meant to carry.

Professional boundaries create emotional safety.

Professionalism Prevents Conflict Before It Escalates

Many conflicts escalate not because of disagreement but because of how disagreement is handled.

Professional behavior:

- De-escalates tension
- Preserves relationships
- Keeps focus on student needs

When professionalism is shared, conflict becomes manageable rather than disruptive.

Alignment thrives in professional environments.

Leadership Sets the Professional Tone

Professionalism cannot be delegated.

Leadership must:

- Model calm under pressure
- Address unprofessional behavior promptly
- Reinforce shared standards consistently

- Protect respectful communication

When leadership tolerates lapses in professionalism, alignment erodes quickly.

Professionalism must be modeled to be maintained.

Repair Is a Hallmark of Professionalism

Professionalism includes repair.

When missteps occur:

- Acknowledgment matters
- Apology matters
- Recommitment matters

Repair models accountability and restores trust. Students learn as much from repair as they do from prevention.

Professionalism is demonstrated not by avoiding mistakes but by addressing them responsibly.

Professionalism Is a Skill, Not a Personality Trait

Professionalism is learned, practiced, and reinforced.

It is not:

- A temperament
- A personality type
- A title-based expectation

It is a shared skill set that strengthens alignment when practiced intentionally.

Professionalism grows through reflection and reinforcement.

From Individual Behavior to Collective Culture

When professionalism becomes a shared standard, culture stabilizes.

Adults:

- Respond predictably
- Support one another

- Uphold alignment consistently

Students benefit from environments where adult behavior is steady even during challenge.

Professionalism is the bridge between alignment and culture.

A Daily Commitment

Professionalism is not a one-time expectation.

It must be chosen:

- Daily
- Intentionally
- Collectively

Professionalism is not about perfection.
It is about consistency and care.

Moving Forward

The next chapter shifts focus from individual professionalism to collective identity—examining how alignment grows into a shared culture that students experience across every space.

Because professionalism protects alignment.
But culture sustains it.

Reflection & Application

- How is professionalism modeled during moments of stress in your school?
- Where do lapses most often occur—and why?
- What shared standards would strengthen alignment immediately?

Professionalism is not optional.
It is foundational.

CHAPTER 9

From Individual Classrooms to Collective Culture

C ulture is not created by slogans. It is created by patterns.

Every classroom contributes to culture, but no classroom exists in isolation. Students move through hallways, transitions, shared spaces, and multiple adults every day. What they experience across those moments becomes the school's culture—whether adults define it intentionally or not.

This chapter centers on a defining truth:

Culture is what students experience consistently, not what adults intend collectively.

Why Individual Excellence Is Not Enough

Many schools rely on strong individual educators to carry the weight of culture.

These classrooms feel calm. Expectations are clear. Students know what to expect. But once students leave those spaces, the experience often changes. Expectations shift. Responses vary. Authority feels inconsistent.

This creates a cultural imbalance.

Students learn that behavior is not about values—it is about location.

Individual excellence is valuable, but culture cannot rest on isolated effort. When alignment stops at the classroom door, culture becomes fragmented.

Culture requires continuity.

Students Experience the School as One Continuous Environment

Students do not experience schools in segments.

They experience:

- Arrival
- Transitions
- Hallways
- Common spaces
- Classrooms
- Dismissal

Each moment contributes to their understanding of what the school stands for. When expectations change dramatically across these spaces, students learn to adapt rather than internalize.

Adaptation creates compliance.
Internalization creates ownership.

Culture grows when expectations feel stable everywhere students go.

Culture Is Formed in the Smallest Repeated Moments

Culture is not shaped by what happens occasionally—it is shaped by what happens repeatedly.

Students notice:

- How adults greet them
- How quickly expectations are reinforced
- Whether correction is consistent
- Whether adults support one another

Small moments repeated daily carry more weight than grand initiatives announced occasionally.

Repetition is culture's foundation.

Climate Can Fluctuate—Culture Should Not

Climate reflects how a school feels in a moment.
Culture reflects how a school functions over time.

A school can have a positive climate one day and a strained climate the next. Culture, however, should remain steady—even when emotions fluctuate.

Culture is revealed when:

- Stress increases
- Conflict arises

- Systems are challenged

If alignment holds under pressure, culture is strong.

When Alignment Becomes Identity

When alignment is sustained, it shifts from practice to identity.

Students begin to speak in cultural language:

- "That's not how we do things here."
- "That wouldn't happen at our school."

These statements indicate that expectations are no longer enforced—they are owned.

Culture becomes identity when students protect it themselves.

Shared Beliefs Anchor Culture during Uncertainty

Culture is reinforced by shared adult beliefs.

When adults believe:

- Students deserve consistency
- Behavior is communication
- Accountability builds trust
- Boundaries and relationships coexist

These beliefs guide responses when situations are unclear. Without shared beliefs, alignment weakens during uncertainty.

Beliefs fill the gaps where policies cannot.

Transitions Are the Culture Test

Transitions expose culture quickly.

Hallways, lunchrooms, entry points, and dismissal reveal whether expectations are shared or situational. When adults respond differently in these spaces, students sense the inconsistency immediately.

Culture is not strongest where adults are most comfortable—it is strongest where alignment holds in shared spaces.

If Adults Do Not Define Culture, Students Will

When culture is undefined, students create their own norms.

They decide:

- What behavior is acceptable
- Where boundaries truly exist
- Whose authority matters

This is not rebellion—it is adaptation to ambiguity.

Adults must define culture intentionally, or students will define it informally.

Leadership Turns Alignment into Culture

Alignment becomes culture through leadership protection.

Leadership sustains culture by:

- Reinforcing expectations across spaces
- Addressing drift early

- Supporting adults who uphold alignment
- Modeling consistency under pressure

Culture does not survive on momentum alone. It requires guardianship.

Collective Accountability Makes Culture Durable

Culture weakens when accountability is individual.

When adults hold one another accountable respectfully:

- Alignment strengthens
- Trust deepens
- Expectations stabilize

Collective accountability ensures culture does not depend on a few strong personalities.

Culture must belong to everyone.

Student Experience Is the Most Honest Measure

Culture should always be measured through student experience.

Ask:

- Do students experience consistency across spaces?
- Do they trust adult follow-through?
- Do expectations feel fair and predictable?

Student experience reveals culture more honestly than adult perception.

A Shift worth Making

This chapter calls for a shift from isolated excellence to shared responsibility.

Strong classrooms matter—but collective culture determines sustainability.

When adults move together, culture follows.

Moving Forward

The next chapter focuses on leadership—not as authority alone, but as protection.

Because alignment becomes culture only when it is guarded.

Reflection & Application

- Where does culture feel strongest in your school— and why?
- Where does inconsistency weaken student trust?
- What adult behaviors are repeated often enough to define culture?

Culture is not built by accident.
It is built by aligned adults—every day.

CHAPTER 10

Leadership That Protects Alignment

Alignment does not collapse in dramatic moments.
It fades in unguarded ones.

Schools rarely lose alignment because adults stop caring. They lose it because leadership underestimates how fragile alignment is in demanding environments. When alignment is not actively protected, it is slowly reshaped by convenience, pressure, and silence.

This chapter is grounded in a defining truth:

Alignment becomes culture only when leadership treats it as something worth protecting—daily, visibly, and without compromise.

Leadership Is the Keeper of What Matters Most

Leadership is not simply about direction.
It is about preservation.

Leaders do not just introduce expectations—they safeguard them. In schools, alignment is one of the most valuable assets, yet it is also one of the most vulnerable.

Leadership preserves alignment by:

- Defending clarity when confusion creeps in
- Reinforcing consistency when fatigue sets in
- Holding standards when pressure mounts

When leadership fails to preserve alignment, it is not replaced with flexibility—it is replaced with fragmentation.

Why Alignment Always Needs a Guardian

Alignment exists in tension with reality.

Reality includes:

- Exhaustion

- Staffing shortages
- Behavioral challenges
- Parent pressure
- Time constraints

In these conditions, alignment is often the first thing sacrificed in the name of efficiency or peacekeeping.

Leadership must act as a guardian—someone willing to protect alignment even when doing so is uncomfortable.

What is not guarded will be reshaped by circumstance.

Protection Is a Moral Decision, Not a Technical One

Protecting alignment is not just operational—it is ethical.

When leadership allows inconsistency:

- Students experience unfairness
- Adults experience confusion
- Culture becomes unpredictable

Every time leadership chooses convenience over consistency, students receive a message—often unintentionally—that expectations are flexible based on circumstance.

Leadership decisions shape student trust.

=

Alignment Is Lost Through Small Compromises

Alignment is rarely abandoned outright.

It is chipped away by small decisions:

- Allowing exceptions without explanation
- Ignoring minor professional lapses
- Failing to address subtle undermining
- Choosing silence to avoid discomfort

Each compromise feels insignificant. Together, they redefine culture.

Leadership must recognize that small compromises accumulate into large cultural shifts.

The Courage to Be Consistent

Protecting alignment requires courage.

It requires leaders to:

- Say no when it would be easier to say yes
- Hold standards when emotions are high
- Maintain expectations even when challenged

Consistency is often mistaken for rigidity. In truth, it is reliability.

Students thrive in environments where adults know what to expect from leadership.

Leadership Presence Is Cultural Reinforcement

Leadership does not protect alignment from a distance.

Presence matters.

When leaders are visible during:

- Transitions
- Conflict

- High-stress moments

They communicate that expectations are not conditional.

Presence reinforces alignment without speeches or directives.

When Leadership Wavers, Culture Shifts

Staff watch leadership closely—not just for instruction, but for permission.

When leadership:

- Overlooks inconsistency
- Avoids difficult conversations
- Sends mixed signals

Adults interpret this as flexibility—or approval.

Leadership behavior gives silent permission for drift.

Protecting the Adults Who Hold the Line

One of the most critical leadership responsibilities is protection of adults.

When staff enforce expectations, maintain professionalism, and stay aligned under pressure, they must be supported—especially when pushback comes from students, parents, or peers.

When adults feel exposed for upholding standards, alignment collapses quickly.

Protection builds trust.
Trust sustains consistency.

Addressing Drift without Creating Fear

Protection does not mean intimidation.

Effective leaders:

- Address drift privately
- Focus on clarity, not character
- Separate behavior from identity

The goal is not compliance through fear—but alignment through understanding.

Correction handled with dignity preserves morale while restoring consistency.

Leadership and Repair Are Inseparable

Even protected alignment will experience strain.

What matters is leadership response.

Strong leaders:

- Name misalignment honestly
- Reset expectations clearly
- Model accountability publicly

Repair teaches adults and students that alignment matters enough to restore.

Avoiding repair communicates that alignment is optional.

Consistency Is the Currency of Leadership Trust

Trust is built when leadership is predictable.

When staff know:

- Expectations will not shift suddenly
- Standards will be applied fairly
- Support will follow aligned action

They act with confidence.

Inconsistent leadership creates hesitation. Hesitation weakens culture.

Alignment Cannot Be Outsourced

Committees, frameworks, and initiatives can support alignment—but they cannot replace leadership ownership.

Alignment requires:

- Authority
- Visibility
- Decision-making

- Willingness to intervene

Leadership may distribute responsibility—but it must retain accountability.

Ownership anchors culture.

Reframing Leadership as Stewardship

Leadership is not about power—it is about stewardship.

Stewards protect what others depend on.

In schools, students depend on:

- Predictability
- Fairness
- Adult unity

Leadership safeguards these conditions through alignment.

When leaders protect alignment, they protect students.

A Daily, Intentional Choice

Protecting alignment is not a one-time initiative.

It is a daily decision to:

- Reinforce expectations
- Address drift
- Support aligned adults
- Model professionalism

Alignment survives not because it is announced—but because it is defended.

Moving Forward

The next chapter explores how alignment is tested during seasons of change—and how schools can remain unified without resisting growth.

Because change is inevitable.
But misalignment does not have to be.

Reflection & Application

- Where alignment might be eroding quietly in your school?
- What compromises have become routine?
- How does leadership respond when alignment is inconvenient?

Alignment endures when leadership chooses courage over convenience—every day.

CHAPTER 11

When Change Tests Unity

C hange is inevitable in schools.
Disunity is not.

Schools are built on movement—new initiatives, new expectations, new leadership, new systems, and new student needs. While change is often necessary for growth, it is also the moment when alignment is most vulnerable. What feels cohesive during stable periods is often strained when transition begins.

This chapter rests on a central truth:

Change does not break alignment—lack of clarity and protection during change does.

When clarity is preserved, alignment can survive even significant shifts.

Why Change Feels Destabilizing—even when it's Right

Change disrupts familiarity.

Adults begin to ask:

- What still matters most?
- What expectations remain non-negotiable?
- Will accountability look the same?
- Who decides now?

When these questions are unanswered, adults default to personal judgment rather than shared agreement. This is not resistance—it is an attempt to regain stability.

Change creates uncertainty.
Uncertainty tests alignment.

The Emotional Reality of Transition

Change is not just procedural—it is personal.

Adults often experience:

- Fear of losing competence

- Fatigue from constant adaptation
- Skepticism rooted in past failed initiatives
- Anxiety about evaluation under new systems

When these emotions go unacknowledged, they manifest as withdrawal, frustration, or quiet resistance. When acknowledged, they can be navigated with professionalism and trust.

Leadership must address emotion without allowing it to dictate standards.

Change Reveals What Was Already Fragile

Change does not create misalignment—it exposes it.

During transition:

- Communication gaps widen
- Inconsistent expectations become visible
- Power dynamics intensify
- Trust is tested

Alignment that existed only during calm seasons often fractures under pressure. Alignment that was built intentionally has a greater chance of holding.

Change reveals the strength of what was already built.

The High Cost of Silence during Change

Silence during change is not neutral.

When adults are not informed:

- Rumors spread
- Anxiety increases
- Assumptions replace clarity

Even when leaders do not yet have answers, communication matters. Honest updates—even incomplete ones—build more trust than silence.

Clarity reduces fear.
Silence multiplies it.

Leadership Presence Is Non-Negotiable During Transition

During change, leadership presence becomes stabilizing.

Effective leaders:

- Are visible and accessible
- Communicate frequently
- Reaffirm expectations repeatedly
- Name what remains consistent

Leadership absence during transition communicates uncertainty—even when none is intended.

Presence anchors alignment.

Protecting the Non-Negotiable

Change invites experimentation—but alignment requires boundaries.

During transition:

- Instructional approaches may shift
- Systems may evolve

- Processes may be refined

What must remain stable?

- Professional conduct
- Shared language
- Behavioral expectations
- Adult unity

When non-negotiable shift without explanation, alignment fractures quickly.

Why Support Roles Experience Change First—and Hardest

Paraprofessionals, teaching assistants, and support staff often feel change before others.

They may:

- Receive information late
- Be excluded from planning
- Experience unclear expectations

This creates immediate misalignment. When support roles are uncertain, students experience inconsistency.

Alignment requires inclusive communication across all roles—not just leadership teams.

Understanding Resistance as Information

Resistance is often mislabeled.

In reality, resistance frequently signals:

- Lack of clarity
- Fear of failure
- Absence of voice
- Change fatigue

When leaders listen without defensiveness, resistance becomes information rather than opposition.

Alignment transforms resistance into readiness.

Students Absorb Adult Uncertainty Immediately

Students feel adult change before they understand it.

They notice:

- Shifts in tone
- Inconsistent enforcement
- Adult hesitation

Students need:

- Predictable expectations
- Calm adult responses
- Reassurance through consistency

When adults remain aligned during change, students remain regulated. When adults fracture, students carry the instability.

Student experience should guide every leadership decision during transition.

Unity without Unanimity

Unity does not require agreement.

It requires:

- Respectful dialogue
- Public reinforcement of direction

- Private space for questioning

Adults can challenge ideas without undermining unity.
Public division during change weakens trust quickly.

Protect unity publicly.
Process disagreement privately.

Pacing Change to Protect Culture

Speed can damage alignment.

Effective leaders:

- Introduce change in phases
- Revisit expectations frequently
- Monitor adult response
- Adjust communication intentionally

Slow does not mean resistant.
It means sustainable.

Culture must be protected while growth occurs.

Leadership's Defining Choice during Change

Every transition presents a choice.

Leaders can:

- Prioritize speed and risk fragmentation
- Or protect unity while guiding progress

The strongest schools choose progress **with** alignment—not progress at alignment's expense.

Change as a Test of Values

Change tests whether stated values are operational or aspirational.

During transition:

- Do expectations remain fair?
- Does professionalism hold?
- Is student experience protected?

Alignment that holds during change becomes culture that endures.

Moving Forward

The next chapter addresses what happens when alignment breaks—and how schools can intentionally repair trust, clarity, and direction.

Because breakdowns will happen.

What defines a school is how it repairs them.

Reflection & Application

- How has past change affected unity in your school?
- Where did uncertainty create misalignment?
- What non-negotiable must be protected during future transitions?

Change is unavoidable.
Alignment is a choice.

CHAPTER 12

Repairing Alignment after Breakdown

Alignment does not disappear because adults fail. It disappears when breakdowns are ignored.

Even the strongest schools experience moments of misalignment. Pressure accumulates. Emotions rise. Communication falters. Decisions are made quickly. Fatigue clouds judgment. These realities do not signal failure—they signal humanity.

What separates schools that fracture from schools that grow stronger is not whether breakdowns occur, but **whether repair is intentional**.

This chapter is grounded in a defining truth:

Repair is not weakness. It is evidence that alignment matters enough to restore.

Why Breakdown Is Not a Leadership Failure

Breakdown is inevitable in human systems.

Schools are complex environments shaped by:

- Constant decision-making
- Emotional labor
- Competing priorities
- Limited time
- High accountability

Expecting alignment to remain flawless under these conditions is unrealistic. Breakdown does not indicate poor leadership. **Ignoring breakdown does.**

Alignment fails when leaders mistake silence for resolution.

The Silent Damage of Unrepaired Alignment

When misalignment goes unaddressed, it does not disappear—it settles.

Unrepaired breakdown leads to:

- Quiet resentment
- Uneven enforcement
- Passive resistance
- Erosion of trust
- Adult withdrawal into silos

Over time, the message becomes clear: expectations are negotiable, and alignment is optional.

Students feel this instability long before adults name it.

How Breakdown Actually Shows Up in Schools

Alignment breakdown rarely announces itself.

More often, it appears as:

- Adults no longer using shared language
- "That's not my issue" responses
- Increased side conversations
- Inconsistent follow-through
- Hesitation to address behavior

These are not personality issues. They are cultural signals.

Breakdown ignored becomes the new normal.

Repair Begins With Courageous Naming

Repair cannot begin without acknowledgment.

Effective leaders name breakdown by:

- Identifying what shifted
- Clarifying what was affected
- Re-centering shared expectations

Naming does not assign blame—it restores clarity.

Avoiding acknowledgment communicates that alignment is no longer a priority.

Why Repair Feels Risky—and Why It Matters

Repair requires vulnerability.

It asks leaders to:

- Admit missteps
- Revisit decisions
- Clarify inconsistencies
- Engage uncomfortable conversations

Avoidance feels safer in the moment. But over time, avoidance costs credibility, trust, and culture.

Courage restores alignment.
Comfort delays it.

Repair Is a Collective Responsibility

Alignment does not break in isolation.

Repair requires:

- Collective reflection
- Shared recommitment
- Open dialogue

When repair is imposed rather than engaged, it lacks ownership. When adults participate in repair, alignment strengthens.

Repair works best when it is done **with** people, not **to** them.

Separating Intent, Impact, and Expectation

One of the most important repair skills is distinguishing between:

- **Intent** – what was meant
- **Impact** – what occurred
- **Expectation** – what must happen moving forward

Effective repair:

- Honors intent without excusing harm
- Centers impact without personalizing blame
- Reasserts expectations clearly

Impact—not intent—must guide repair decisions.

Leadership Models Repair First

Leadership sets the tone for restoration.

When leaders:

- Acknowledge misalignment
- Apologize when appropriate
- Reaffirm expectations clearly

They model accountability without defensiveness.

This modeling teaches staff and students that alignment is not fragile—it is resilient.

Repair Requires Action, Not Just Conversation

Words alone do not restore alignment.

Repair must include:

- Re-establishing shared language
- Consistent reinforcement of expectations
- Visible leadership support
- Clear follow-through

Consistency after repair rebuilds trust faster than explanation alone.

Repairing Relationships While Holding the Line

Repair does not mean lowering standards.

It means:

- Addressing relational harm
- Rebuilding trust
- Reasserting boundaries

Strong schools do not choose between relationships and expectations—they honor both.

Repair without clarity creates confusion.
Clarity without repair creates resentment.

When Repair Is Met With Resistance

Not all adults respond to repair immediately.

Some resist because of:

- Fatigue
- Distrust

- Past unresolved breakdowns

Leadership must respond with:

- Continued clarity
- Consistent reinforcement
- Support paired with accountability

Repair is an invitation—but alignment still requires commitment.

Students Experience Adult Repair—Even Indirectly

Students notice when adults repair alignment.

They sense:

- Reduced tension
- Increased consistency
- Calm adult behavior

Repair restores emotional safety—even when students are not directly involved.

Students trust adults who can address conflict responsibly.

Turning Breakdown into Strength

When repair is intentional, breakdown becomes growth.

Repair leads to:

- Stronger trust
- Clearer expectations
- Deeper adult unity
- More resilient culture

What could have fractured alignment instead strengthens it.

Repair does not erase the breakdown—it redeems it.

Making Repair a Cultural Expectation

This chapter calls for a cultural shift.

Alignment will strain.
Breakdowns will occur.

What defines a school is not the absence of breakdown—
but the **presence of repair**.

When repair becomes expected, alignment becomes resilient.

Moving Forward

The next chapter explores how alignment becomes sustainable—through systems, habits, and shared ownership that reduce breakdown and strengthen culture over time.

Because the strongest schools do not just repair alignment.

They reinforce it.

Reflection & Application

- Where has alignment broken down recently in your school?
- Was it acknowledged—or avoided?
- What would intentional repair look like in your context?

Alignment is not proven by perfection.
It is proven by restoration.

WHEN ADULTS ALIGN

CHAPTER 13

Sustaining Alignment over Time

A lignment is not sustained by passion. It is sustained by practice.

Most schools can create alignment temporarily—after a training, a crisis, a reset, or a strong start to the year. The real work is not building alignment once. The real work is **keeping it alive when urgency fades, attention shifts, and routines return**.

This chapter is grounded in a defining truth:

Alignment endures when it becomes the default way adults operate—not a goal they revisit only when things go wrong.

Why Alignment Naturally Fades

Alignment rarely disappears abruptly.

It fades gradually when:

- Competing initiatives pull focus

- Daily pressures overshadow reflection
- Turnover disrupts continuity
- Fatigue reduces intentionality

Without reinforcement, alignment becomes something adults *remember* rather than something they *practice*. Memory is unreliable. Practice is durable.

Sustained alignment requires design—not hope.

From Agreement to Architecture

Alignment often begins with agreement.

But agreement alone is fragile.

Sustainability requires architecture:

- Structures that reinforce expectations
- Habits that normalize consistency
- Systems that correct drift automatically

When alignment is embedded into how decisions are made, how communication occurs, and how expectations are reinforced, it no longer depends on motivation.

Architecture outlasts enthusiasm.

Habits: The Quiet Protectors of Alignment

Habits carry alignment when attention wanes.

Shared habits may include:

- Using common language instinctively
- Responding predictably to behavior
- Addressing drift early and calmly
- Reinforcing expectations without escalation

When habits are shared, alignment survives individual differences in style, energy, or experience.

Habits remove guesswork.

Embedding Alignment into Daily Routines

Alignment must live inside daily routines—not outside them.

This includes:

- How meetings begin and end
- How expectations are referenced
- How concerns are raised
- How leadership communicates priorities

When alignment is woven into routines, it becomes invisible—but powerful.

Invisible systems shape visible culture.

Onboarding as Cultural Preservation

Every new adult enters a culture already in motion.

If alignment is not made explicit during onboarding:

- New staff rely on observation
- Inconsistencies multiply
- Culture dilutes quickly

Sustaining alignment requires intentional onboarding that explains not just *what* is done—but *why* it matters.

New staff do not weaken culture.

Unclear culture does.

Protecting Alignment through Turnover and Transition

Turnover is inevitable. Alignment loss is not.

Sustainable alignment requires:

- Clear documentation of expectations
- Leadership consistency across personnel changes
- Collective ownership beyond individual champions

When alignment belongs to the system, it survives changes in staffing and leadership.

Culture that depends on people disappears when they do.

Leadership Reinforcement as a Rhythm

Leadership reinforcement must become routine—not reactive.

This includes:

- Predictable visibility
- Consistent messaging
- Timely correction of drift
- Public affirmation of aligned behavior

Reinforcement does not require speeches or reminders—it requires repetition.

What leadership reinforces consistently becomes permanent.

Preventing Drift Before It Requires Repair

Sustained alignment reduces the need for major repair.

Leaders who:

- Notice subtle shifts
- Address small inconsistencies early
- Revisit expectations regularly

Prevent minor drift from becoming systemic breakdown.

Maintenance is leadership wisdom.

Collective Accountability as Cultural Insurance

Alignment is strongest when accountability is shared.

This includes:

- Adults respectfully holding one another to standards
- Teams naming drift without defensiveness
- Leadership welcoming feedback on consistency

When accountability is collective, alignment does not depend on hierarchy.

Culture is strongest when everyone protects it.

Student Experience as the Ultimate Measure

Sustained alignment must always be measured through student experience.

Ask repeatedly:

- Do students experience predictability across spaces?

- Do expectations feel fair and consistent?
- Does adult behavior feel steady—even under stress?

Students are the most honest indicators of whether alignment is holding.

When student experience shifts, alignment needs attention.

Reflection as Preventive Maintenance

Reflection keeps alignment alive.

This may include:

- Regular staff reflection prompts
- Leadership check-ins on consistency
- Team conversations about shared practice

Reflection is not a pause from work—it is part of the work.

What is reflected on is retained.

Alignment Is a Posture, Not a Project

Alignment is never finished.

It is a posture adults adopt daily.

It requires:

- Ongoing awareness
- Willingness to adjust
- Commitment to consistency over convenience

Schools that sustain alignment understand that maintenance is excellence—not extra effort.

From Alignment to Institutional Memory

When alignment is sustained long enough, it becomes institutional memory.

It shapes:

- How new adults learn expectations
- How conflict is handled
- How decisions are made
- How students experience school

Alignment becomes legacy when it outlives individuals and initiatives.

A Final Commitment to Endurance

This chapter calls for a final commitment.

Alignment is not maintained by effort alone—but by intention made routine.

When adults:

- Protect consistency
- Share ownership
- Reinforce expectations daily

Alignment becomes durable.

And when alignment endures, culture becomes strong enough to carry students—year after year.

Reflection & Application

- Where is alignment currently sustained by habit— and whereby effort alone?
- What systems could replace reminders?

- What routines could reinforce alignment automatically?

Alignment is not proven by enthusiasm.
It is proven by endurance.

EPILOGUE

The Work Continues

Thereis no finish line for alignment.

There will be days when it feels strong—when adults move together with clarity, professionalism, and trust. There will also be days when it feels strained—when stress rises, patience thins, and consistency takes effort.

Both are part of the work.

Alignment is not proven on easy days.
It is revealed on the hard ones.

Progress, Not Perfection

This book never promised perfection.

It offered something more realistic—and more powerful: **progress through intention.**

Every time adults:

- Choose shared language over personal preference
- Respond with professionalism instead of emotion
- Repair instead of retreat
- Protect unity instead of convenience

Alignment is strengthened.

Progress may be quiet.
But it is meaningful.

The Students Will Tell the Story

Students may never say the word *alignment*.

But they will feel it.

They will feel it in:

- Predictable expectations
- Calm adult responses
- Fair accountability
- Consistent care

They will feel safer.

They will feel clearer.

They will feel supported.

And in time, that feeling becomes trust.

Alignment Is a Living Commitment

Alignment must be renewed.

Each year brings:

- New students
- New staff
- New challenges
- New opportunities

What remains constant is the responsibility to move together.

Alignment is not something you *complete*.

It is something you *practice*.

A Final Encouragement

When the work feels heavy, remember this:

You are not aligning for systems.
You are aligning for students.

For the student who needs consistency to feel safe.
For the student who needs clarity to regulate.
For the student who needs adults to move together to believe that fairness exists.

Every aligned choice matters.

Carry This Forward

Let alignment:

- Guide conversations
- Shape decisions
- Anchor leadership
- Protect culture

And when alignment strains—as it will—return to the basics:

- Shared language

- Professionalism
- Repair
- Unity

That is where strength is rebuilt.

The Invitation Remains

Alignment is not demanded.
It is invited.

And every adult who accepts that invitation helps create a school where students can thrive—not just academically, but emotionally and socially as well.

The work continues.

And it matters.

When adults align, students do more than succeed.
They believe.

CONCLUSION

The Work That Remains

Alignment is not a theory.
It is a responsibility.

Throughout this book, one truth has remained consistent: students do not experience schools through policies, titles, or intentions. They experience schools through **adult behavior**—what adults say, what adults tolerate, and how adults move together when things are difficult.

When adults align, students feel it.

They feel it in the consistency of expectations.
They feel it in the calm of adult responses.
They feel it in the fairness of consequences.
They feel it in the trust that adults will do what they say they will do.

Alignment is not abstract.
It is personal.

This Was Never About Perfection

This book was never about perfect classrooms, flawless leadership, or unanimous agreement.

It was about:

- Shared responsibility
- Collective consistency
- Professional unity
- Student-centered decision-making

Alignment does not mean everyone thinks the same.
It means everyone protects the same priorities.

Schools do not need perfect adults.
They need **aligned adults**.

Why Adult Alignment Matters More Than Ever

Students are navigating a world filled with inconsistency, uncertainty, and unpredictability.

Schools should not add to that instability.

When adults are misaligned:

- Students feel confused
- Behavior escalates
- Trust erodes
- Culture weakens

When adults are aligned:

- Students feel safe
- Expectations are clear
- Accountability feels fair
- Learning becomes possible

Adult alignment is not optional work.
It is foundational work.

The Quiet Power of Consistency

Much of alignment happens quietly.

It happens when:

- Adults support one another publicly
- Expectations are reinforced calmly

- Drift is addressed early
- Repair happens when breakdown occurs

Students may never name alignment—but they live inside its impact every day.

Consistency is the loudest message adults send.

Alignment Is a Daily Choice

Alignment is not something a school *achieves*.
It is something a school *chooses*—daily.

It is chosen when:

- Adults use shared language
- Professionalism holds under pressure
- Leadership protects consistency
- Repair is prioritized over avoidance

Every day offers opportunities to drift—or to realign.

Alignment is sustained by what adults choose repeatedly.

The Charge to Adults

If there is one charge this book leaves behind, it is this:

Move together. Even when it's uncomfortable.
Especially when it's hard.

Students are watching how adults handle disagreement, stress, and change. They are learning not just content—but character, communication, and conflict resolution.

What do adults model that students internalize?

The Charge to Leaders

Leadership is not about enforcing alignment—it is about **protecting it**.

Protect it by:

- Being visible
- Being consistent
- Being courageous
- Being willing to repair

Alignment does not survive on authority.

It survives on stewardship.

The Charge to the School Community

Alignment belongs to everyone.

It is strengthened when:

- Adults hold one another accountable with respect
- Support roles are included and valued
- Expectations are shared across spaces
- Student experience remains the priority

Culture is not built by individuals working hard in isolation.

It is built by adults choosing unity over convenience.

A Final Word

Students do not need adults to be louder.

They need adults to be clearer.

WHEN ADULTS ALIGN

They do not need stricter rules.
They need consistent ones.

They do not need perfection.
They need alignment.

When adults align, schools stabilize.
When schools stabilize, students thrive.

This is the work.
This is the responsibility.
This is the invitation.

Choose alignment.
Protect it.
Sustain it.

The students are counting on it.

REFLECTION

Reflection Page 1: Alignment Check

Take a moment to reflect honestly on the current state of alignment in your school.

- Where do adults feel most aligned?

_____

_____

_____

- Where does misalignment most often appear?

_____

_____

_____

- How does adult alignment (or misalignment) show up in student behavior?

Reflection Page 2: Shared Language

Language shapes direction.

- What phrases or language are consistently used across adults in your school?

  _____

  _____

  _____

- Where does language differ—and how might that impact students?

  _____

  _____

  _____

- What shared language would immediately strengthen clarity and consistency?

_____

_____

_____

Reflection Page 3: Professionalism under Pressure

Professionalism matters most when things are difficult.

- How do adults typically respond under stress in
  your school?

  _____

  _____

  _____

- What behaviors strengthen professionalism during
  challenging moments?

  _____

  _____

  _____

- What behaviors unintentionally weaken alignment?

Reflection Page 4: Culture beyond the Classroom

Culture is experienced everywhere.

- Where does culture feel strongest outside of classrooms?

- Where does inconsistency most often appear (hallways, transitions, and common areas)?

- What adult actions could improve consistency across spaces?

_____

_____

_____

Reflection Page 5: Leadership & Protection

Alignment requires protection.

- How does leadership currently reinforce alignment?

_____

_____

_____

- Where alignment might be drifting quietly?

_____

_____

_____

- What leadership actions would strengthen consistency immediately?

_____

_____

_____

Reflection Page 6: Change & Unity

Change tests alignment.

- How has change impacted adult unity in the past?

  _____

  _____

  _____

- What helped protect alignment during transition?

  _____

  _____

  _____

- What lessons should guide future change efforts?

  _____

  _____

  _____

Reflection Page 7: Repair & Restoration

Breakdowns are inevitable. Repair is intentional.

- Where has alignment broken down recently?

  _____

  _____

  _____

- Was repair addressed—or avoided?

  _____

  _____

  _____

- What would intentional repair look like moving forward?

  _____

  _____

  _____

Reflection Page 8: Sustainability

Alignment must outlast urgency.

- What systems currently sustain alignment in your school?

  _____

  _____

  _____

- Where is alignment still dependent on individuals?

  _____

  _____

  _____

- What habits or routines could make alignment automatic?

  _____

  _____

  _____

Reflection Page 9: Personal Commitment

Alignment begins with individual responsibility.

- What is one behavior you will commit to that supports alignment?

_____

_____

_____

- What is one habit you will work to change?

_____

_____

_____

- How will you contribute to protecting alignment for students?

_____

_____

_____

Reflection Page 10: Collective Commitment

Use this space for a shared commitment—individually or as a team.

We commit to protecting alignment by...

_____

_____

_____

Signatures (optional):

_____

_____

_____

Date: _____

_____

Alignment is not proven by agreement.
It is proven by consistency.

SIGNATURE ALIGNMENT PLEDGE

Alignment is not an event.

It is a promise we keep—together.

This pledge affirms our shared responsibility to act with clarity, consistency, and unity in service of students.

THE ALIGNMENT PLEDGE

By signing this pledge, I affirm that I will:

- Act in alignment with shared expectations and collective standards
- Use consistent language that supports clarity for students
- Maintain professionalism in words, actions, and decisions
- Support colleagues publicly and resolve concerns privately

- Participate honestly in repair when alignment is strained
- Place student experience above personal preference
- Protect alignment during challenge, change, and pressure

I understand that alignment is not about agreement—it is about responsibility.

INDIVIDUAL PLEDGE

I pledge to uphold alignment as a daily practice and a professional responsibility.

Name (Printed):

_____

Signature:

_____

Role/Position:

_____

Date:

_____

COLLECTIVE / SCHOOL PLEDGE (Optional)

As a team or school community, we pledge to move together with consistency, clarity, and purpose—protecting alignment so students experience stability, fairness, and trust.

School / Team Name:

_____

Representative Signature:

_____

Date:

_____

Alignment is not proven by words.
It is proven by how we show up—together.

WHEN ADULTS ALIGN

WHEN ADULTS ALIGN

www.ingramcontent.com/pod-product-compliance
Lightning Source LLC
Chambersburg PA
CBHW060421130626
46555CB00005B/2165